Spiral to Infinity Steve Allen

"Fractal images are often made up of small images-within-images, constantly repeating and going smaller and smaller." – **Steve Allen**

Investigations
IN NUMBER, DATA, AND SPACE®

Editorial offices: Glenview, Illinois • Parsippany, New Jersey • New York, New York
Sales offices: Boston, Massachusetts • Duluth, Georgia
Glenview, Illinois • Coppell, Texas • Sacramento, California • Mesa, Arizona

The Investigations curriculum was developed by TERC, Cambridge, MA.

This material is based on work supported by the National Science Foundation ("NSF") under Grant No.ESI-0095450. Any opinions, findings, and conclusions or recommendations expressed in this material are those of the author(s) and do not necessarily reflect the views of the National Science Foundation.

ISBN: 0-328-24088-5

ISBN: 978-0-328-24088-3

2 3 4 5 6 7 8 9 10-V057-15 14 13 12 11 10 09 08 07

CC:N1

Math Words and Ideas

Number and Operations

Patterns and Functions

Data and Probability

Contents

Geometry

Measurement

Contents

Games

The **Student Math Handbook** is a reference book. It has two sections.

Math Words and Ideas

These pages illustrate important math words and ideas that you have been learning about in math class. You can use these pages to think about or review a math topic. Important terms are identified and related problems are provided.

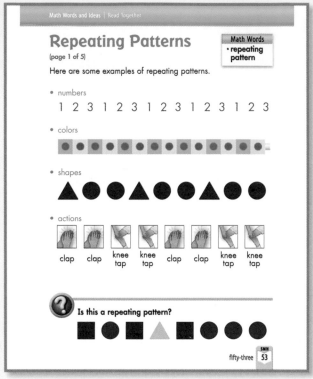

▲ Student Math Handbook, p. 53

Games

You can use the Games pages to go over game rules during class or at home. They also list the materials and recording sheets needed to play each game.

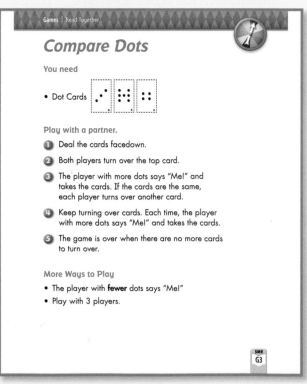

▲ Student Math Handbook, p. G3

Daily Practice and Homework pages list
useful *Student Math Handbook* (SMH) pages.

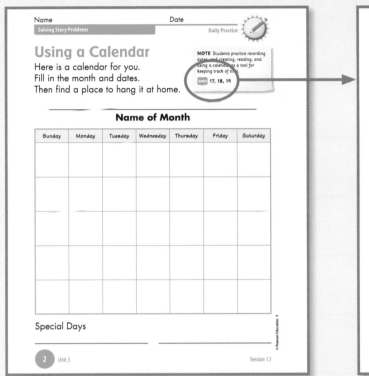

▲ Student Activity Book, Unit 3, p. 2

▲ Student Math Handbook, p. 17

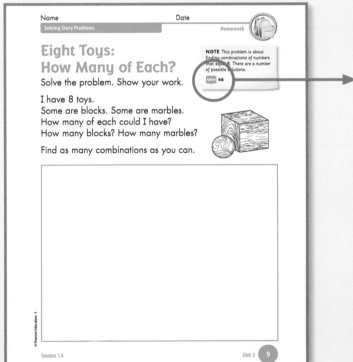

▲ Student Activity Book, Unit 3, p. 9

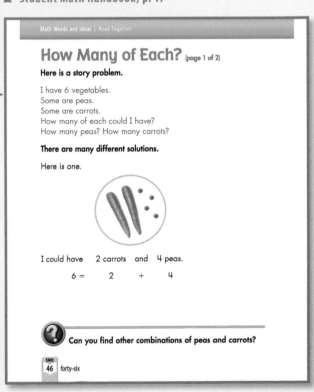

▲ Student Math Handbook, p. 46

Numbers

0	zero	
1	one	■
2	two	■■
3	three	■■■
4	four	■■■■
5	five	■■■■■
6	six	■■■■■□
7	seven	■■■■■□□
8	eight	■■■■■□□□
9	nine	■■■■■□□□□

10	ten	
11	eleven	10 + ▪ =11
12	twelve	10 + ▪▪ =12
13	thirteen	10 + ▪▪▪ =13
14	fourteen	10 + ▪▪▪▪ =14
15	fifteen	10 + ▪▪▪▪▪ =15
16	sixteen	10 + ▪▪▪▪▪▪ =16
17	seventeen	10 + ▪▪▪▪▪▪▪ =17
18	eighteen	10 + ▪▪▪▪▪▪▪▪ =18
19	nineteen	10 + ▪▪▪▪▪▪▪▪▪ =19

20	twenty	
21	twenty-one	20 +
22	twenty-two	20 +
23	twenty-three	20 +
24	twenty-four	20 +
25	twenty-five	20 +
26	twenty-six	20 +
27	twenty-seven	20 +
28	twenty-eight	20 +
29	twenty-nine	20 +

30	thirty	
31	thirty-one	30 + ▪
32	thirty-two	30 + ▪▪
33	thirty-three	30 + ▪▪▪
34	thirty-four	30 + ▪▪▪▪
35	thirty-five	30 + ▪▪▪▪▪
36	thirty-six	30 + ▪▪▪▪▪
37	thirty-seven	30 + ▪▪▪▪▪▪▪
38	thirty-eight	30 + ▪▪▪▪▪▪▪▪
39	thirty-nine	30 + ▪▪▪▪▪▪▪▪▪

40	forty	
41	forty-one	40 + ▪
42	forty-two	40 + ▪▪
43	forty-three	40 + ▪▪▪
44	forty-four	40 + ▪▪▪▪
45	forty-five	40 + ▪▪▪▪▪
46	forty-six	40 + ▪▪▪▪▫
47	forty-seven	40 + ▪▪▪▪▫▫
48	forty-eight	40 + ▪▪▪▪▫▫▫
49	forty-nine	40 + ▪▪▪▪▫▫▫▫

50	fifty	
51	fifty-one	50 + ▪
52	fifty-two	50 + ▪▪
53	fifty-three	50 + ▪▪▪
54	fifty-four	50 + ▪▪▪▪
55	fifty-five	50 + ▪▪▪▪▪
56	fifty-six	50 + ▪▪▪▪▪▫
57	fifty-seven	50 + ▪▪▪▪▪▫▫
58	fifty-eight	50 + ▪▪▪▪▪▫▫▫
59	fifty-nine	50 + ▪▪▪▪▪▫▫▫▫

60	sixty	
61	sixty-one	60 + ▪
62	sixty-two	60 + ▪▪
63	sixty-three	60 + ▪▪▪
64	sixty-four	60 + ▪▪▪▪
65	sixty-five	60 + ▪▪▪▪▪
66	sixty-six	60 + ▪▪▪▪▪▫
67	sixty-seven	60 + ▪▪▪▪▪▫▫
68	sixty-eight	60 + ▪▪▪▪▪▫▫▫
69	sixty-nine	60 + ▪▪▪▪▪▫▫▫▫

70	seventy	
71	seventy-one	70 + ▪
72	seventy-two	70 + ▪▪
73	seventy-three	70 + ▪▪▪
74	seventy-four	70 + ▪▪▪▪
75	seventy-five	70 + ▪▪▪▪▪
76	seventy-six	70 + ▪▪▪▪▪▫
77	seventy-seven	70 + ▪▪▪▪▪▫▫
78	seventy-eight	70 + ▪▪▪▪▪▫▫▫
79	seventy-nine	70 + ▪▪▪▪▪▫▫▫▫

80	eighty	
81	eighty-one	80 + ▪
82	eighty-two	80 + ▪▪
83	eighty-three	80 + ▪▪▪
84	eighty-four	80 + ▪▪▪▪
85	eighty-five	80 + ▪▪▪▪▪
86	eighty-six	80 + ▪▪▪▪▪▫
87	eighty-seven	80 + ▪▪▪▪▪▫▫
88	eighty-eight	80 + ▪▪▪▪▪▫▫▫
89	eighty-nine	80 + ▪▪▪▪▪▫▫▫▫

90	ninety	
91	ninety-one	90 + ▨
92	ninety-two	90 + ▨▨
93	ninety-three	90 + ▨▨▨
94	ninety-four	90 + ▨▨▨▨
95	ninety-five	90 + ▨▨▨▨▨
96	ninety-six	90 + ▨▨▨▨▨▨
97	ninety-seven	90 + ▨▨▨▨▨▨▨
98	ninety-eight	90 + ▨▨▨▨▨▨▨▨
99	ninety-nine	90 + ▨▨▨▨▨▨▨▨▨

100	one hundred	
101	one hundred one	100 + ▫
102	one hundred two	100 + ▫▫
103	one hundred three	100 + ▫▫▫
104	one hundred four	100 + ▫▫▫▫
105	one hundred five	100 + ▫▫▫▫▫
106	one hundred six	100 + ▫▫▫▫▫▫
107	one hundred seven	100 + ▫▫▫▫▫▫▫
108	one hundred eight	100 + ▫▫▫▫▫▫▫▫
109	one hundred nine	100 + ▫▫▫▫▫▫▫▫▫

Calendar

Math Words
• calendar

A calendar is a tool. It shows days and months in a year. A calendar can also show important days and events.

days of the week

month

year

September 2009

Sunday	Monday	Tuesday	Wednesday	Thursday	Friday	Saturday
		1	**2** First Day of School	**3**	**4**	**5**
6	**7**	**8** Family Breakfast	**9**	**10**	**11**	**12**
13	**14**	**15**	**16**	**17** Trip to the Park	**18**	**19**
20	**21**	**22** First Day of Fall	**23**	**24**	**25**	**26**
27	**28**	**29**	**30**			

What happens on Tuesday, September 8?
What day of the week is the first day of school?
When does fall begin?

Calendar: Days of the Week

Math Words
- days
- week
- hours

There are 7 days in a week.

Sunday	Monday	Tuesday	Wednesday	Thursday	Friday	Saturday

**What day comes before Wednesday?
What day comes after Friday?**

There are 24 hours in a day.

A day is the time between bedtime tonight and bedtime tomorrow.

One day lasts from sunrise to sunrise.

**What day is today? What day is tomorrow?
What day was yesterday?**

Calendar: Months of the Year

There are 12 months in a year.
This calendar shows all 12 months in 2009.

January						
S	M	T	W	T	F	S
				1	2	3
4	5	6	7	8	9	10
11	12	13	14	15	16	17
18	19	20	21	22	23	24
25	26	27	28	29	30	31

February						
S	M	T	W	T	F	S
1	2	3	4	5	6	7
8	9	10	11	12	13	14
15	16	17	18	19	20	21
22	23	24	25	26	27	28

March						
S	M	T	W	T	F	S
1	2	3	4	5	6	7
8	9	10	11	12	13	14
15	16	17	18	19	20	21
22	23	24	25	26	27	28
29	30	31				

April						
S	M	T	W	T	F	S
			1	2	3	4
5	6	7	8	9	10	11
12	13	14	15	16	17	18
19	20	21	22	23	24	25
26	27	28	29	30		

May						
S	M	T	W	T	F	S
					1	2
3	4	5	6	7	8	9
10	11	12	13	14	15	16
17	18	19	20	21	22	23
24	25	26	27	28	29	30
31						

June						
S	M	T	W	T	F	S
	1	2	3	4	5	6
7	8	9	10	11	12	13
14	15	16	17	18	19	20
21	22	23	24	25	26	27
28	29	30				

July						
S	M	T	W	T	F	S
			1	2	3	4
5	6	7	8	9	10	11
12	13	14	15	16	17	18
19	20	21	22	23	24	25
26	27	28	29	30	31	

August						
S	M	T	W	T	F	S
						1
2	3	4	5	6	7	8
9	10	11	12	13	14	15
16	17	18	19	20	21	22
23	24	25	26	27	28	29
30	31					

September						
S	M	T	W	T	F	S
		1	2	3	4	5
6	7	8	9	10	11	12
13	14	15	16	17	18	19
20	21	22	23	24	25	26
27	28	29	30			

October						
S	M	T	W	T	F	S
				1	2	3
4	5	6	7	8	9	10
11	12	13	14	15	16	17
18	19	20	21	22	23	24
25	26	27	28	29	30	31

November						
S	M	T	W	T	F	S
1	2	3	4	5	6	7
8	9	10	11	12	13	14
15	16	17	18	19	20	21
22	23	24	25	26	27	28
29	30					

December						
S	M	T	W	T	F	S
		1	2	3	4	5
6	7	8	9	10	11	12
13	14	15	16	17	18	19
20	21	22	23	24	25	26
27	28	29	30	31		

Some months have 30 days. Some months have 31 days. February has 28 days. Every 4 years, February has 29 days. This is called a *leap year*.

What month comes after April?
What month comes before October?
Find a month with 30 days.

Coins

These coins are used in the United States.
Each coin has a name and a value.

Coin	Name	Value
	penny	1¢ 1 cent
	nickel	5¢ 5 cents
	dime	10¢ 10 cents
	quarter	25¢ 25 cents
	half dollar	50¢ 50 cents

? **Is a bigger coin always worth more?**

Counting (page 1 of 3)

We count to find out how many.
How many blocks? Count to find out.

1   2   3   4   5

There are 5 blocks.

In school, we count:
- days on the calendar
- people

1 2 3   4   5   6   7   8

JANUARY

S	M	T	W	T	F	S
				①	②	③
④	⑤	⑥	⑦	8	9	10
11	12	13	14	15	16	17
18	19	20	21	22	23	24
25	26	27	28	29	30	31

- on the number line

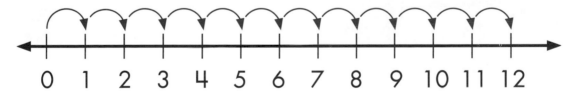

0 1 2 3 4 5 6 7 8 9 10 11 12

When do you count?
What do you like to count?

Counting (page 2 of 3)

When you count, you say one number for each object. You need to keep track of what you are counting. The last number you say is the total. The total tells you how many are in the group.

Look at how some children count.

Math Words
• **total**

Sam touches each button as he counts it.

Rosa puts each button in the cup as she counts it.

Kim arranges the buttons in a row to count.

Max puts them in groups of 2 to double-check.

? **What do you do when you count?**

Counting (page 3 of 3)

Look at these pennies.
They are mixed up.
They are hard to count.

Here are some different ways to organize the pennies
so that they are easier to count.

Which group of pennies is easiest for you to count?

Counting by Groups (page 1 of 2)

You can count more quickly if you count by groups. Each time you say a number, you add another group. Every group must have the same number of objects in it.

Each hand has 5 fingers. You can count by 5s to find the total number of fingers. You say every fifth number when you count by 5s.

Counting fingers by 5s

5   10   15   20

Counting shoes by 2s

2   4   6   8

Counting toes by 10s

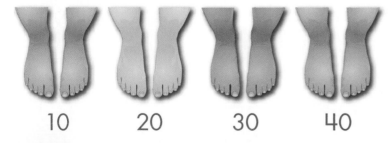

10   20   30   40

How many eyes would 10 people have in all?

Counting by Groups (page 2 of 2)

Here are 23 pennies.

You can count the pennies in different ways.

Counting by 2s

2   4   6   8   10   12   14   16   18   20   22   23

Counting by 5s

5   10   15   20   23

Counting by 10s

10   20   23

  How many different ways can you count 18 pennies?

Number Line

A number line is a tool. It shows numbers in order.

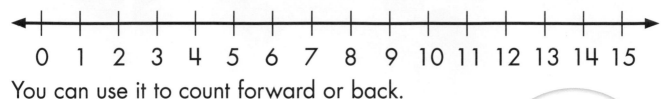

You can use it to count forward or back.

When we count forward,
the numbers go up.

1, 2, 3,
4, 5, 6.

When we count back,
the numbers go down.

5, 4, 3,
2, 1, 0.

 Start with 0 and count to 15.
Start with 12 and count to 0.

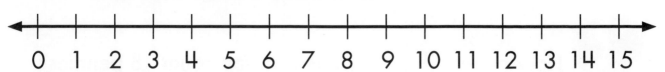

100 Chart (page 1 of 3)

The 100 chart is a tool that shows numbers from 1 to 100, in order. It can help you count, add, and subtract.

column →

row →

1	2	3	4	5	6	7	8	9	10
11	12	13	14	15	16	17	18	19	20
21	22	23	24	25	26	27	28	29	30
31	32	33	34	35	36	37	38	39	40
41	42	43	44	45	46	47	48	49	50
51	52	53	54	55	56	57	58	59	60
61	62	63	64	65	66	67	68	69	70
71	72	73	74	75	76	77	78	79	80
81	82	83	84	85	86	87	88	89	90
91	92	93	94	95	96	97	98	99	100

How many rows are in the 100 chart?
How many numbers are in each row?
How many columns are in the 100 chart?
How many numbers are in each column?

100 Chart (page 2 of 3)

1	2	3	4	5	6	7	8	9	10
11	12	13	14	15	16	17	18	19	20
21	22	23	24	25	26	27	28	29	30
31	32	33	34	35	36	37	38	39	40
41	42	43	44	45	46	47	48	49	50
51	52	53	54	55	56	57	58	59	60
61	62	63	64	65	66	67	68	69	70
71	72	73	74	75	76	77	78	79	80
81	82	83	84	85	86	87	88	89	90
91	92	93	94	95	96	97	98	99	100

"In each row, the 10s number stays the same and the 1s number goes up by 1."

"In each column, the 10s number goes up by 1 and the 1s number stays the same."

What patterns do you notice?

100 Chart (page 3 of 3)

Some of the numbers on this 100 chart are missing.

1	2	3	4	5	6		8		10
	12	13	14	15	16	17	18	19	20
21	22		24	25	26	27	28	29	30
31	32	33	34				38	39	40
41	42	43	44	45	46	47	48	49	50
51		53	54	55	56	57	58	59	60
61	62	63	64	65	66	67			
71	72	73	74	75	76	77	78	79	80
81	82		84	85	86	87	88	89	90
91	92	93	94	95	96		98	99	100

What numbers are missing?
How do you know?

200 Chart

Here is a 200 chart.

1	2	3	4	5	6	7	8	9	10
11	12	13	14	15	16	17	18	19	20
21	22	23	24	25	26	27	28	29	30
31	32	33	34	35	36	37	38	39	40
41	42	43	44	45	46	47	48	49	50
51	52	53	54	55	56	57	58	59	60
61	62	63	64	65	66	67	68	69	70
71	72	73	74	75	76	77	78	79	80
81	82	83	84	85	86	87	88	89	90
91	92	93	94	95	96	97	98	99	100
101	102	103	104	105	106	107	108	109	110
111	112	113	114	115	116	117	118	119	120
121	122	123	124	125	126	127	128	129	130
131	132	133	134	135	136	137	138	139	140
141	142	143	144	145	146	147	148	149	150
151	152	153	154	155	156	157	158	159	160
161	162	163	164	165	166	167	168	169	170
171	172	173	174	175	176	177	178	179	180
181	182	183	184	185	186	187	188	189	190
191	192	193	194	195	196	197	198	199	200

How is it the same as the 100 chart?
How is it different from the 100 chart?
Find 76. Where is 176?

Counting Forward

You can use the number line and the 100 chart
to count forward from any number. You do not have
to start with 1. Max starts with 8 and counts to 14.

"8, 9, 10, 11, 12, 13, 14."

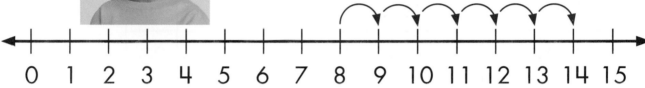

1	2	3	4	5	6	7	8	9	10
11	12	13	14	15	16	17	18	19	20
21	22	23	24	25	26	27	28	29	30
31	32	33	34	35	36	37	38	39	40
41	42	43	44	45	46	47	48	49	50
51	52	53	54	55	56	57	58	59	60
61	62	63	64	65	66	67	68	69	70
71	72	73	74	75	76	77	78	79	80
81	82	83	84	85	86	87	88	89	90
91	92	93	94	95	96	97	98	99	100

Use the 100 chart to count from 38 to 52.

Counting Back

You can use the number line and the 100 chart to count back from any number. Rosa counts back from 33 to 24.

"33, 32, 31, 30, 29, 28, 27, 26, 25, 24."

1	2	3	4	5	6	7	8	9	10
11	12	13	14	15	16	17	18	19	20
21	22	23	24	25	26	27	28	29	30
31	32	33	34	35	36	37	38	39	40
41	42	43	44	45	46	47	48	49	50
51	52	53	54	55	56	57	58	59	60
61	62	63	64	65	66	67	68	69	70
71	72	73	74	75	76	77	78	79	80
81	82	83	84	85	86	87	88	89	90
91	92	93	94	95	96	97	98	99	100

? **Use the number line to count back from 15 to 9.**

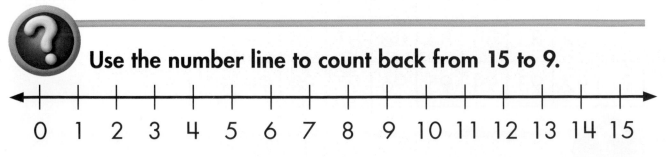

Solving Addition Problems (page 1 of 5)

Here is a story problem:

Kim has 3 crayons. Sam gives her 4 more. How many crayons does Kim have now?

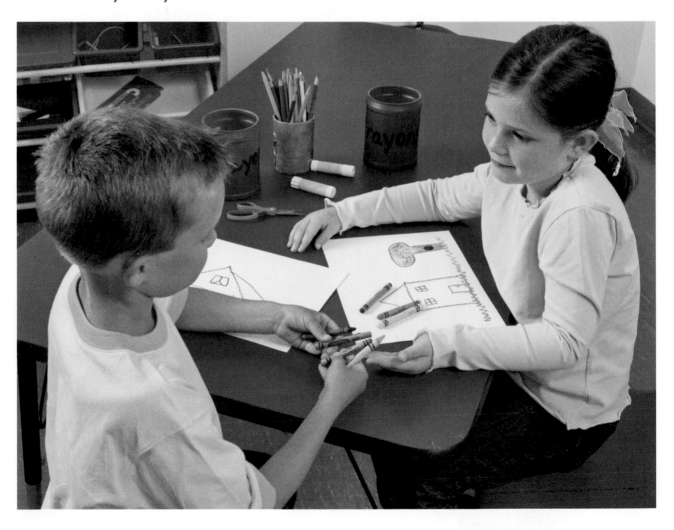

 Does Kim have more crayons at the beginning or the end of the story?

Solving Addition Problems (page 2 of 5)

Here is the story:

Kim has 3 crayons. Sam gives her 4 more.
How many crayons does Kim have now?

There are many ways to solve this problem.
Here is what some children did:

Paula took 3 crayons. Then she took 4. Then she counted.	Pei drew 4 lines. Then he drew 3 lines. He counted on from 4.

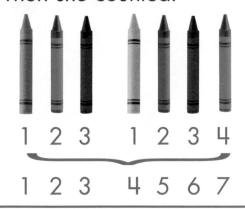

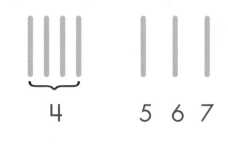

I know that $3 + 3 = 6$.
So $3 + 4$ is one more.

? How would you solve this problem?

Solving Addition Problems (page 3 of 5)

Math Words
- **equation**
- **plus**
- **equal to**
- **addend**
- **sum**
- **equal sign**

Kim has 3 crayons. Sam gives her 4 more.
Now Kim has 7 crayons.

Here are 2 equations for this problem.

3 + 4 = 7

3 plus 4 is equal to 7.

7 = 3 + 4

7 is equal to 3 plus 4.

3 and 4 are the addends. 7 is the total, or the sum.

The equal sign shows that 3 + 4 is the same amount as 7.

Solving Addition Problems (page 4 of 5)

Here is a story problem:

Rosa has 8 shells.
Sam gives her 3 more shells.
Max gives her 2 more shells.
How many shells does Rosa have now?

 Does Rosa have more shells at the beginning or at the end of the story?

Solving Addition Problems (page 5 of 5)

There are many ways to solve this problem.
This is what some children did:

Paul drew and counted each shell.

Isabel counted on from 8 on a number line.

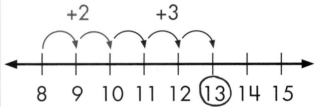

Vic used a combination of 10.

$8 + 2 = 10$

Then he counted on.

11, 12, 13

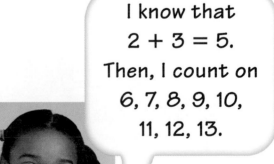

I know that $2 + 3 = 5$. Then, I count on 6, 7, 8, 9, 10, 11, 12, 13.

How would you solve the problem?

Solving Subtraction Problems (page 1 of 5)

Here is a story problem:

Sam had 10 pennies.
He spent 6 on a pencil.
How many pennies did he have left?

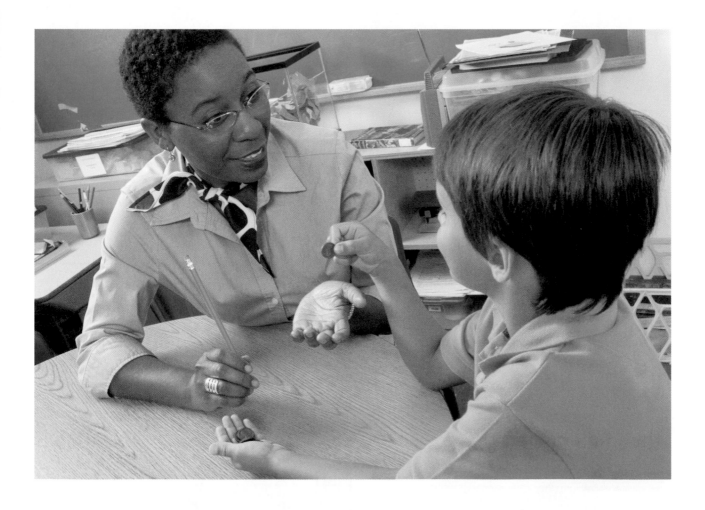

 Does Sam have more pennies at the beginning of the story or at the end?

Solving Subtraction Problems (page 2 of 5)

There are many ways to solve this problem.
This is what some children did.

Kim drew 10 circles and crossed out 6. Then she counted how many were left.

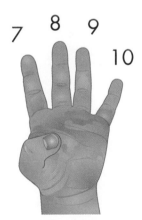

Vic counted back 6 on a number line.

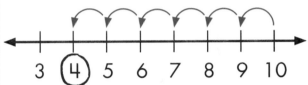

Max counted up from 6 to 10.

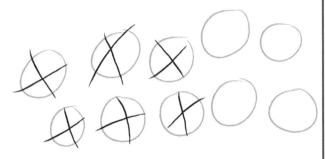

Then he counted his fingers: 1, 2, 3, 4

Rosa used what she knew about addition combinations.

I know that 4 + 6 = 10. So, 10 − 6 must be 4.

 How would you solve the problem?

Solving Subtraction Problems (page 3 of 5)

Math Words
- **minus**
- **equals**
- **difference**

Sam had 10 pennies.
He spent 6 on a pencil.
Now he has 4.

Here is an equation for this problem.

$$10 - 6 = 4$$

10 minus 6 equals 4

The difference between 10 and 6 is 4.

The equal sign shows that $10 - 6$ is the same amount as 4.

Solving Subtraction Problems (page 4 of 5)

Here is a story problem.

Max had 15 pennies in his piggy bank. He took out 7 pennies to buy a pencil. How many pennies are still in his piggy bank?

 Does Max have more pennies in his bank at the beginning of the story or at the end?

Solving Subtraction Problems (page 5 of 5)

Max had 15 pennies in his piggy bank.
He took out 7 pennies to buy a pencil.
How many pennies are still in his piggy bank?

There are many ways to solve this problem.
This is what some children did.

Tina counted out 15 and took 7 away. Then she counted how many were left.

Stacy used a number line and counted back.

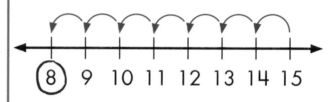

Leah counted up from 7 to 15. It was 8.

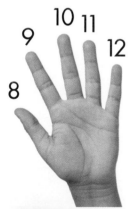 

Paul used what he knew about addition combinations.

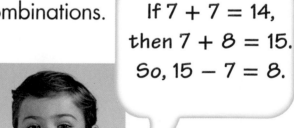

If 7 + 7 = 14, then 7 + 8 = 15. So, 15 − 7 = 8.

 How would you solve the problem?

Math Symbols

> greater than, more than	**6** 🌙🌙🌙🌙🌙 🌙 **>** **4** ✏️✏️✏️✏️
	There are 6 moons. There are 4 pencils.
	There are more moons than pencils.
	6 is greater than 4.
	6 > 4
< less than, fewer than	**3** 🌙🌙🌙 **<** **5** 🌸🌸🌸🌸🌸
	There are 3 moons. There are 5 flowers.
	There are fewer moons than flowers.
	3 is less than 5.
	3 < 5

Using Math Symbols

(page 1 of 2)

+ plus sign addition sign	 4 + 3 = 7 4 plus 3 is equal to 7. 4 plus 3 equals 7.
− minus sign subtraction sign	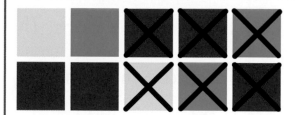 10 − 6 = 4 10 minus 6 is equal to 4. 10 minus 6 equals 4.
= equal sign	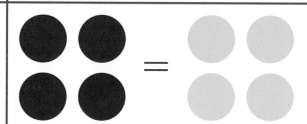 4 = 4 4 is the same as 4. 4 is equal to 4. 4 equals 4.

Using Math Symbols

(page 2 of 2)

An equation uses numbers and symbols to show what is happening in a math problem.

$$8 + 2 = 10 \qquad 10 - 4 = 6$$

Here are two ways to write addition or subtraction problems.

$$\begin{array}{r} 8 \\ +\ 2 \\ \hline 10 \end{array} \qquad \text{is the same as} \qquad 8 + 2 = 10$$

$$10 - 4 = 6 \qquad \text{is the same as} \qquad \begin{array}{r} 10 \\ -\ 4 \\ \hline 6 \end{array}$$

How Many of Each? (page 1 of 2)

Here is a story problem.

I have 6 vegetables.
Some are peas.
Some are carrots.
How many of each could I have?
How many peas? How many carrots?

There are many different solutions.

Here is one.

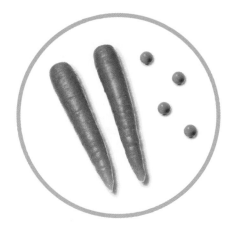

I could have   2 carrots   and   4 peas.

$$6 = \quad 2 \quad + \quad 4$$

Can you find other combinations of peas and carrots?

How Many of Each? (page 2 of 2)

Here are some children's solutions.

Edgar: 5 peas and 1 carrot

$$5 + 1 = 6$$

Allie: 3 peas and 3 carrots

$$3 + 3 = 6$$

Nicky: 2 peas and 4 carrots

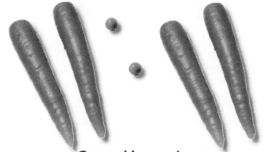

$$2 + 4 = 6$$

Talisa: 4 peas and 2 carrots

$$4 + 2 = 6$$

Lyle: 1 pea and 5 carrots

$$1 + 5 = 6$$

 If there were 7 vegetables, how many peas and carrots could there be? Find as many combinations as you can.

Combinations of 10 (page 1 of 2)

Here are some ways to make 10.

$3 + 7 = 10$

$5 + 5 = 10$

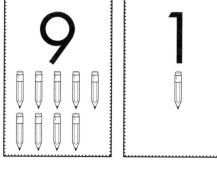

$9 + 1 = 10$

$6 + 4 = 10$

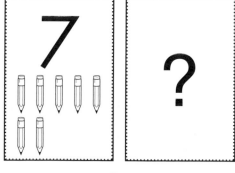

$7 +$ ___?___ $= 10$

What card do you need to make 10?
What other ways can you make 10 with 2 cards?
Can you make 10 with 3 cards?

Combinations of 10 (page 2 of 2)

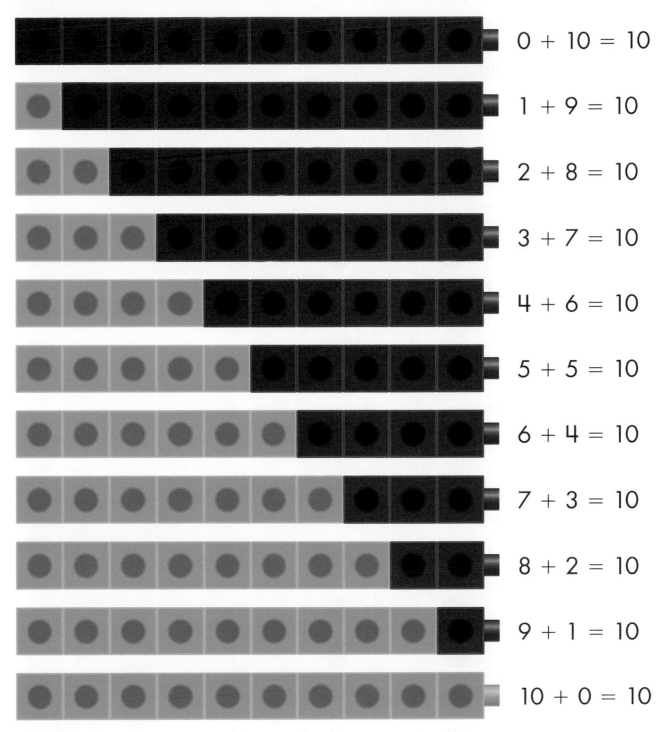

0 + 10 = 10

1 + 9 = 10

2 + 8 = 10

3 + 7 = 10

4 + 6 = 10

5 + 5 = 10

6 + 4 = 10

7 + 3 = 10

8 + 2 = 10

9 + 1 = 10

10 + 0 = 10

What do you notice about these combinations of 10?

Using Combinations of 10

(page 1 of 2)

Here is a problem.

$$8 + 5 = \underline{\ ?\ }$$

Think about combinations of 10 to solve this problem.

Max says, "Think about Ten-Frames."

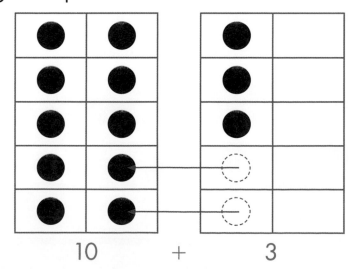

"If you take 2 from the 5 and give it to the 8, you've got 10 plus 3. That is 13."

$$8 + 5 = 10 + 3 = 13$$

Using Combinations of 10

(page 2 of 2)

8 + 5 = __?__

Rosa says, "Think about cubes."

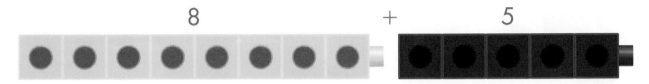

"Break 5 into a 2 and a 3."

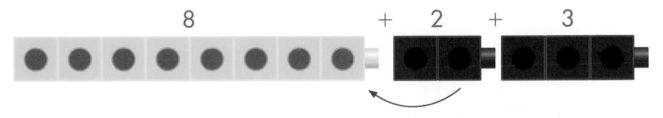

"8 plus 2 is 10. Plus 3 more is 13."

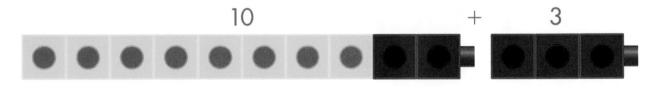

8 + 5 = 10 + 3 = 13

Today's Number

Today's Number is 8.
Here are some different ways to make 8.

$$6 + 2 = 8$$

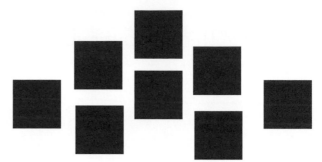

$$8 = 7 + 1$$

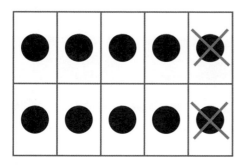

$$10 - 2 = 8$$

$$5 + 3 = 8$$

$$4 + 4 = 8$$

$$2 + 2 + 3 + 1 = 8$$

 What is another way to make 8?

Repeating Patterns

(page 1 of 5)

Here are some examples of repeating patterns.

- numbers

  1 2 3 1 2 3 1 2 3 1 2 3 1 2 3

- colors

- shapes

- actions

  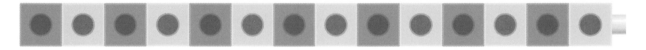

  clap   clap   knee tap   knee tap   clap   clap   knee tap   knee tap

? Is this a repeating pattern?

Repeating Patterns

(page 2 of 5)

The unit is the part of the pattern that repeats.

unit:

1 2 3

pattern:

1 2 3 1 2 3 1 2 3 1 2 3 1 2 3

unit:

pattern:

 What is the unit here?

clap   clap   knee tap   clap   clap   knee tap   clap   clap   knee tap

Repeating Patterns (page 3 of 5)

AB Repeating Patterns

Some repeating patterns look like this:

A B A B A B A B A B A B A B A B

fish   cat   fish   cat   fish   cat

clap   snap   clap   snap   clap   snap   clap   snap

 How are these patterns the same?

Repeating Patterns (page 4 of 5)

ABC Repeating Patterns

Some repeating patterns look like this:

A B C   A B C   A B C   A B C   A B C

1 2 3 1 2 3 1 2 3 1 2 3 1 2 3

| fish | dog | cat | fish | dog | cat |

 How are these patterns the same?

Repeating Patterns (page 5 of 5)

AAB Repeating Patterns

Some repeating patterns look like this:

A A B   A A B   A A B   A A B   A A B

dog   dog   cat   dog   dog   cat

clap   clap   knee   clap   clap   knee   clap   clap   knee
              tap   tap   tap

 How are these patterns the same?

Even and Odd Numbers

Some numbers are even.

These numbers are even.

2   4   6   8   10   12   14   16   18   20

Some numbers are odd.

These numbers are odd.

3   5   7   9   11   13   15   17   19   21

Even and odd numbers make an AB pattern.

1	2	3	4	5	6	7	8	9	10	11
odd	even	odd	even	odd	even	odd	even	odd	even	odd

Is 20 even or odd? Is 19 even or odd?

What Comes Next?

In a repeating pattern, you can determine what comes next.

The pattern unit is one blue cube and one orange cube.

The next cube will be a blue cube.

The pattern unit is one blue triangle, one red circle,

one yellow rectangle.

The next shape will be a yellow rectangle.

If this pattern continues in the same way, what comes next?

What Comes Here?

You can figure out what comes later in a repeating pattern.

If this pattern continues in the same way, what comes here?

If this pattern continues, what comes here?

1 2 3 4 1 2 3 4 1 2 3 4 1 2 3 4 ☐ ☐ ☐ ☐ ?

If this pattern continues in the same way, what comes here?

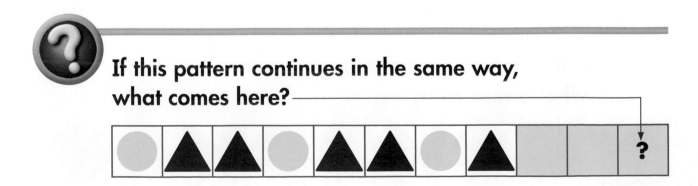

Growing Patterns (page 1 of 3)

Staircase Towers

These staircase towers follow a pattern as they get taller. Each tower has 2 more cubes than the tower before it.

Start with: 2

Step-up: 2

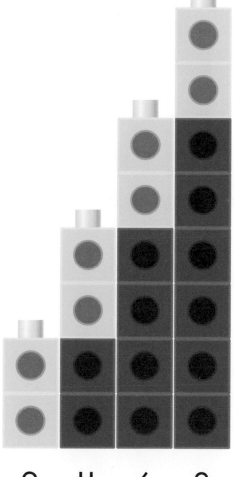

Number of Cubes: 2   4   6   8

If this pattern continues, how many cubes will be in the next tower?

Growing Patterns (page 2 of 3)

Penny Jar

I have one penny in a jar. Every day, I add three more pennies.

My jar looks like this.

1	4	7	10
Start	Day 1	Day 2	Day 3

How many pennies will be in my jar on Day 5?

Growing Patterns (page 3 of 3)

Counting by Groups of 2

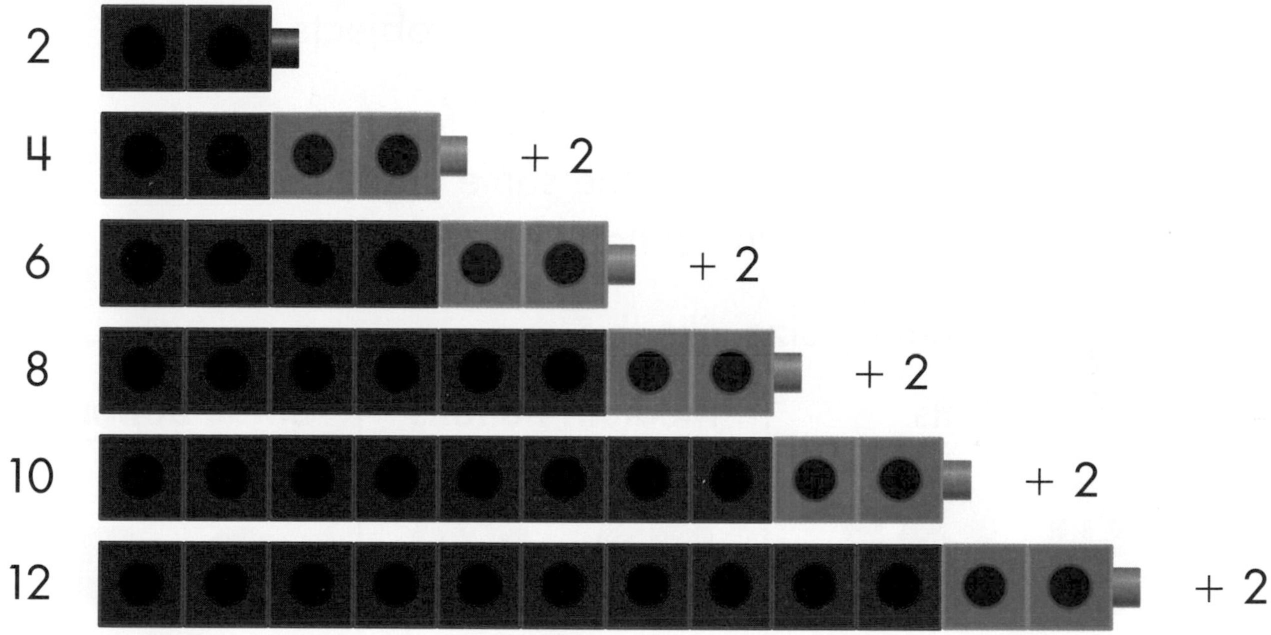

2

4   + 2

6   + 2

8   + 2

10   + 2

12   + 2

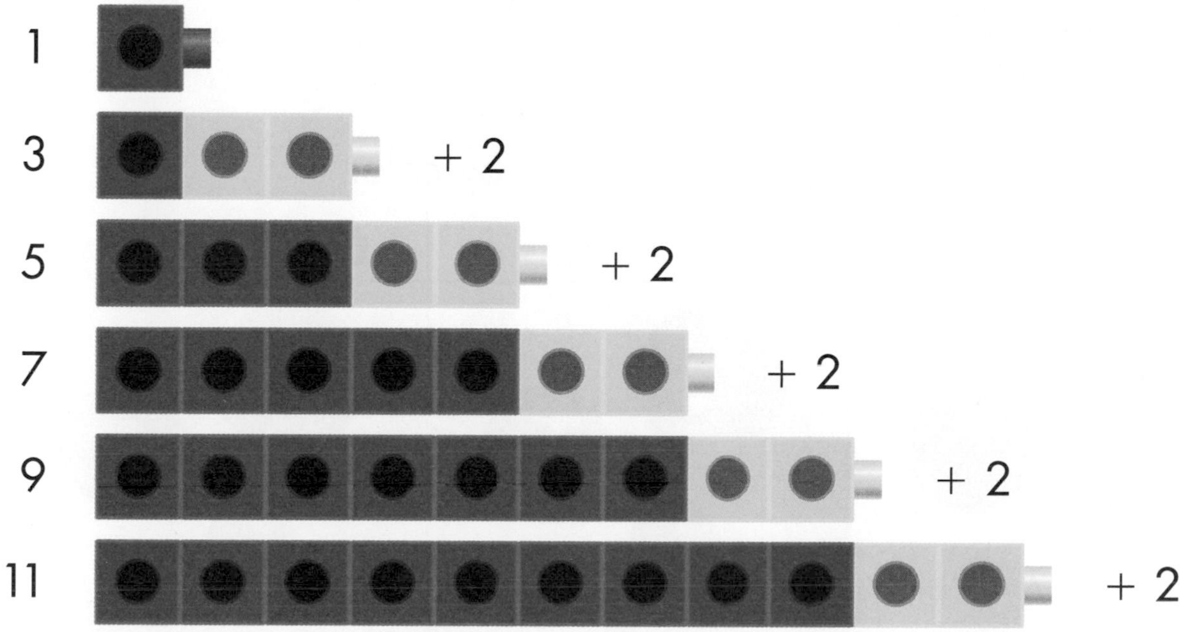

1

3   + 2

5   + 2

7   + 2

9   + 2

11   + 2

Sorting

You can sort data or objects in different ways.
Sorting into groups can show what is the same
and what is different about the data or the objects.

Lyle collected buttons.
He wanted to find out what was the same and
what was different about the buttons.

First he sorted them by size, like this.

Big Buttons	Medium Buttons	Small Buttons

Then he noticed that he could also sort by color.

Red Buttons	Blue Buttons	Orange Buttons

 In what other ways could you sort these buttons?

Data

Data means information. You collect data by asking the same question to a group of people.

Marta wanted to get a dog. Her mother told her that first she needed to learn how to take care of a dog. Marta began by collecting data on who she knew who had a dog.

Marta asked this question:

Do you have a dog?

 What are some things you have collected data about?

Surveys

Math Words
• **survey**

One way to find out what you want to know is to use a survey. A survey is asking a group of people the same question and keeping track of their answers.

Marta's survey

Do you have a dog?

Yes	No
Allie	Bruce
Carol	Teo
Diego	Emilia
Felipe	Leah
Lyle	Paul
Paula	William
Stacy	Libby
	Vic
	Tamika
	Chris
	Nicky
	Isabel
	Toshi

**How many classmates did Marta ask?
Who could Marta ask for advice about how
to take care of a dog?**

Tally Marks

Math Words
• tally mark

Making tally marks is one way to represent data. One tally mark, or line, stands for one answer, or thing, that you are collecting data about. After you make a tally mark for each item, you count them to find the total.

Marta used tally marks to count her data. She made 4 lines. Then she drew a line across the 4 marks to show a group of 5. Here is how Marta counted the answers to her survey question.

Do you have a dog?

Yes	No
5 6, 7	5 10 11, 12, 13

**Look at Marta's data.
How many students do not have a dog?
How many students did Marta survey?**

Representation

A representation of data is a way to show other people what you found out.

Here is Marta's representation:

Dogs	No Dogs
Allie	Bruce
Carol	Teo
Diego	Emilia
Felipe	Leah
Lyle	Paul
Paula	William
Stacy	Libby
	Vic
	Tamika
	Chris
	Nicky
	Isabel
	Toshi

Dear Mom,

I collected data about the kids in my class who have dogs. I found out that 7 kids in my class have dogs.

When I need to know how to take care of my dog, there are 7 kids I can ask for advice. Can I get a dog, please?

Love,
Marta

Geometry

Geometry is the study of shapes.

There are shapes everywhere. We can find shapes in our classroom, at home, on the street, and in the world around us.

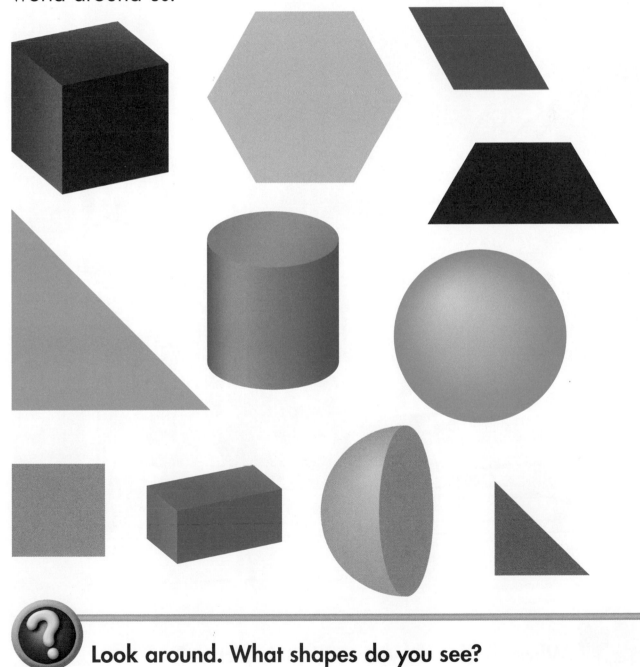

Look around. What shapes do you see?

Shapes in the World

What shapes do you see in this picture?

2-D Shapes

Math Words
• **two-dimensional**

Two-dimensional, or 2-D, shapes are flat. They can be drawn on a sheet of paper or any other flat surface. Here are some 2-D shapes.

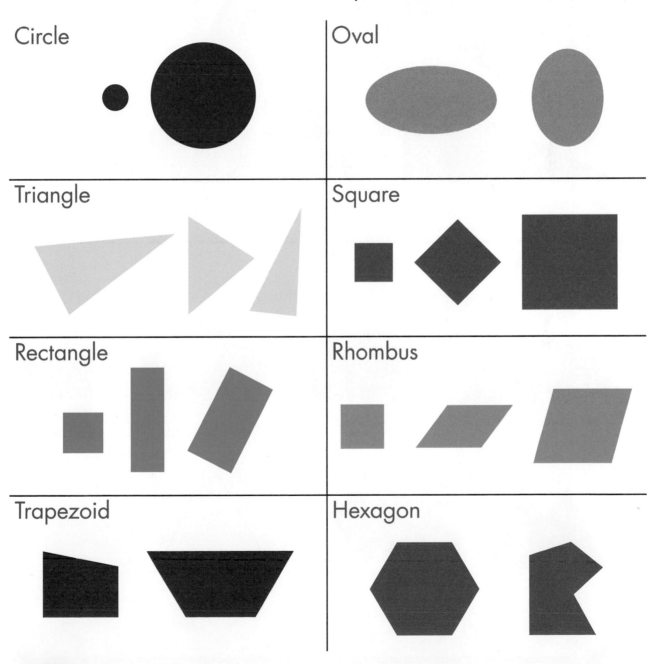

Circle

Oval

Triangle

Square

Rectangle

Rhombus

Trapezoid

Hexagon

Draw some 2-D shapes. What shapes did you draw?

Triangles

These shapes are triangles.

These are **not** triangles.

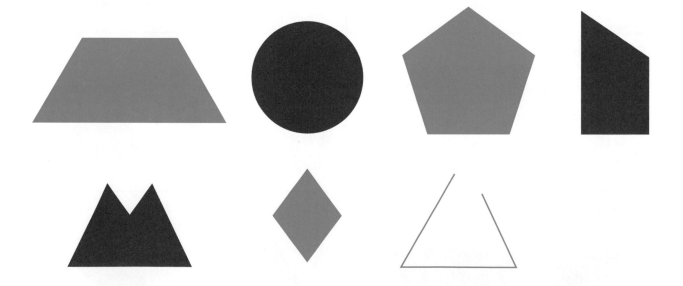

 What is the same about the shapes that are triangles?

Quadrilaterals

These shapes are quadrilaterals.

Math Words
• **quadrilateral**

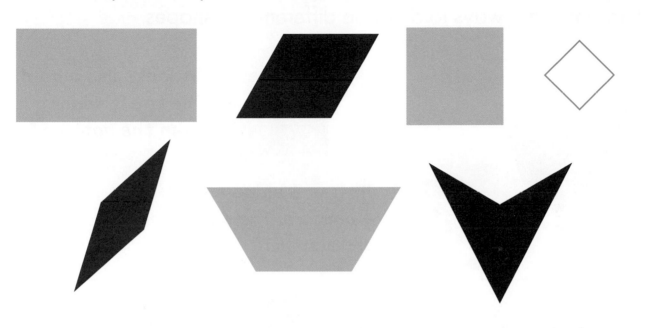

These are **not** quadrilaterals.

 What is the same about the shapes that are quadrilaterals?

Describing 2-D Shapes

You can describe 2-D shapes by how they look.
Here are some ways to describe different 2-D shapes.

"It looks like a bowl. The top is wider than the bottom."

"It has 4 sides and 4 corners. The sides are slanted."

"It's got 3 points. The one on top is very pointy."

"It's a triangle but it's tilted like it's falling over."

"It's like an oval, but there are no curves."

"It looks like a stop sign."

 How would you describe these shapes?

Describing 2-D Shapes: Sides and Vertices

Math Words
- **sides**
- **vertex, vertices (corners)**

2-D shapes have sides and vertices. A lot of first graders call vertices corners. Think about a triangle.

A triangle has 3 sides.

A vertex is the place where 2 sides meet. If there is more than one vertex, they are called vertices.

A triangle has 3 vertices or corners.

How many sides does a quadrilateral have? How many vertices does it have?

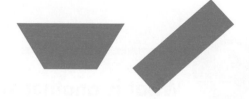

Sorting Shapes (page 1 of 2)

Look at this group of shapes.
How are these shapes the same? How are they different?
Think about different ways you could sort them into groups.

Max sorted these shapes like this.

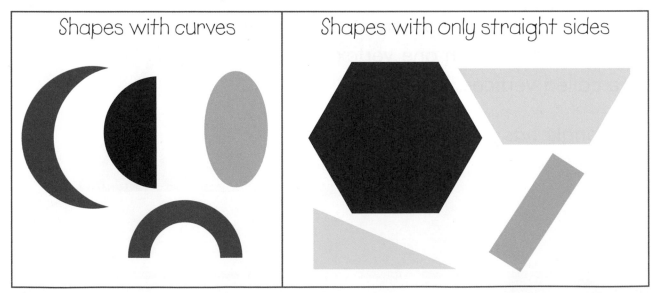

Shapes with curves	Shapes with only straight sides

 What is another way to sort these shapes?

Sorting Shapes (page 2 of 2)

Here's another group of shapes.

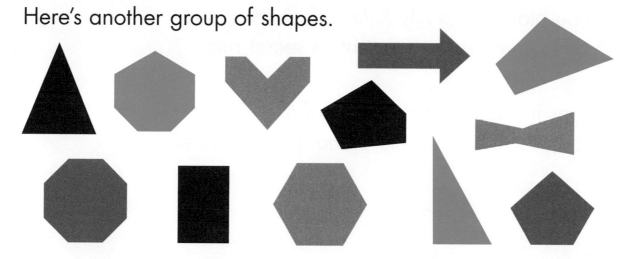

Rosa sorted these shapes like this.

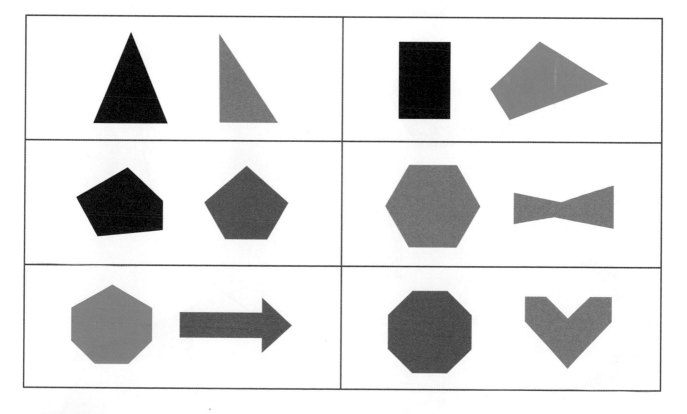

How did Rosa sort the shapes?
What would you name the groups?

Guess My Rule (page 1 of 2)

When you play *Guess My Rule* with shapes, one player picks some shapes that fits a secret rule.

The shapes inside the circle fit Sam's rule.
The shapes outside the circle do not fit Sam's rule.

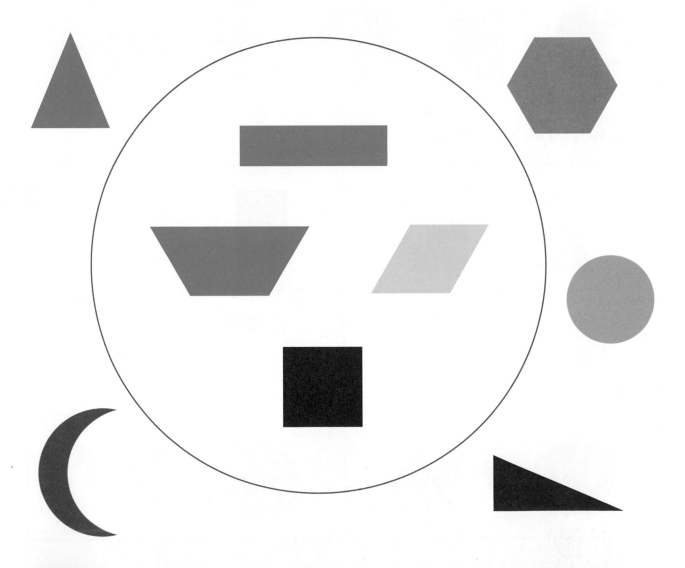

 Can you guess Sam's rule?

Guess My Rule (page 2 of 2)

The shapes inside this circle fit Kim's rule.
The shapes outside the circle do not fit Kim's rule.

 Can you guess Kim's rule?

Filling Shapes with More and Fewer

Shapes can be filled with other shapes. Here is a shape.

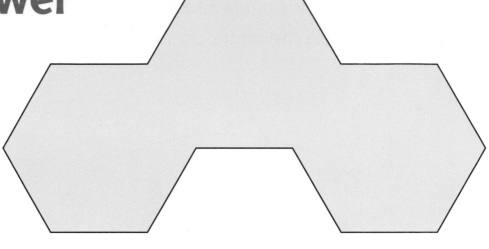

3 hexagons fit into this shape.

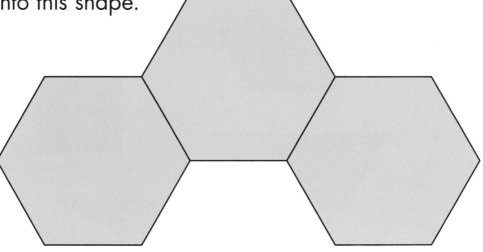

 How many triangles fit into the same shape?

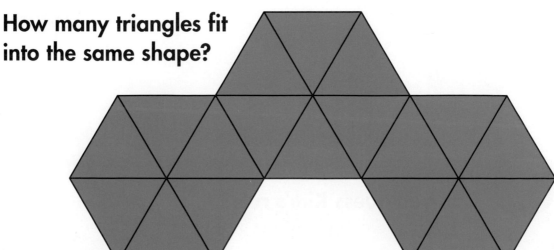

Combining Shapes

You can put shapes together to make other shapes.

Here are some shapes you can make with 2 triangles.

Here are some shapes you can make with
2 rectangles.

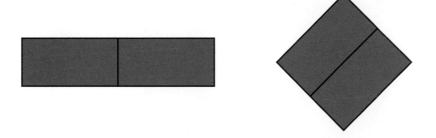

Here are some shapes you can make with
6 triangles.

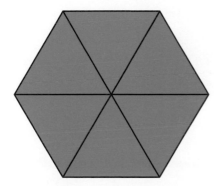 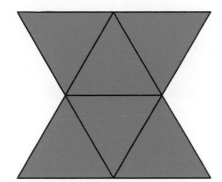

Quilts

Some people use shapes
to make quilts.
Here is one quilt square:

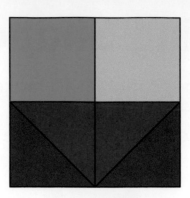

How many times do you see this square in the quilt?

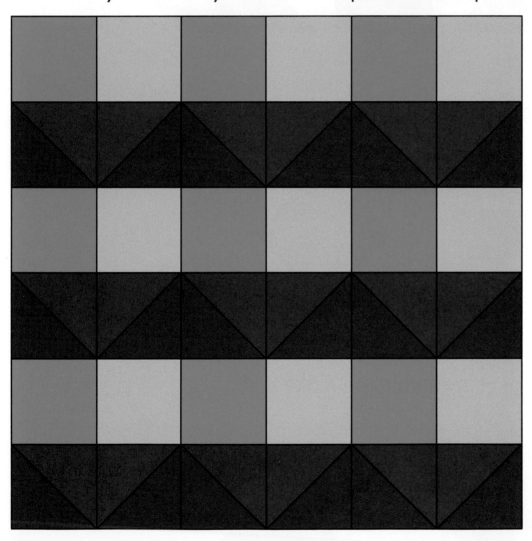

What other shapes are in the quilt?
How many triangles do you see?

3-D Shapes

Three-dimensional, or 3-D, shapes are solid objects. If they are small, you can pick them up and hold them. Here are some 3-D shapes.

Math Words
- **three-dimensional**

Cube

Rectangular Prism

Triangular Prism

Triangular Pyramid

Square Pyramid

Cone

Cylinder

SOUP

Sphere

Look around you. What 3-D shapes do you see?

Drawing 3-D Shapes

It's hard to draw 3-D shapes on paper.

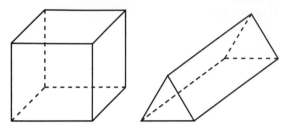

Here are some first-grade drawings of 3-D shapes.

How would you draw a 3-D shape?

Describing 3-D Shapes

You can describe 3-D shapes by how they look.
Here are some ways to describe different 3-D shapes.

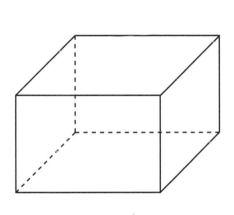

This shape looks like a box.

I see rectangles on the sides.

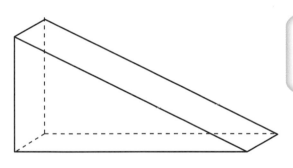

This shape looks like a ramp. It has 2 triangle sides and pointy corners.

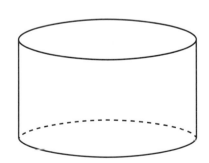

This shape is round like a can. It has a circle on the top and bottom. The sides are curved.

 How would you describe these shapes?

Describing 3-D Shapes: Edges, Faces, and Vertices (Corners)

3-D shapes have faces, edges, and vertices. Think about a cube.

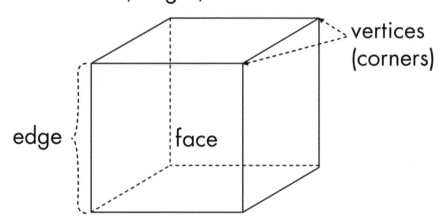

vertices
(corners)

edge

face

An edge is the line or side where 2 faces meet.

A cube has 12 edges.

A face is a 2-D shape on the side of a 3-D shape. On a cube all of the faces are square.

A cube has 6 faces.

A vertex is the point or corner where edges meet.

A cube has 8 vertices, or corners.

What shapes are the faces that you can see on this triangular prism?

Naming 3-D Shapes: Prisms

Math Words
- **prism**
- **rectangular prism**
- **triangular prism**
- **cube**

A prism is a 3-D shape that has only flat faces. These prisms have 2 opposite faces that are the same. These faces are connected by rectangles.

Rectangular Prism

These rectangular prisms have 6 faces.
All of the faces are rectangles.

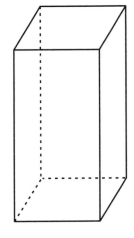
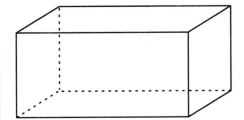
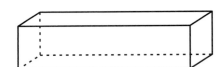

Triangular Prism

These triangular prisms have 2 triangular faces that are connected by 3 rectangles.

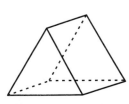
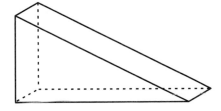

Cube

A cube has 6 faces that are all squares.
A cube is a special kind of rectangular prism.

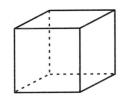

Naming 3-D Shapes

Math Words
- **pyramid**
- **cylinder**
- **sphere**
- **cone**

Here are some other 3-D shapes.

Pyramid
The bottom of a pyramid can be any shape that has straight sides. All of the other faces are triangles.

Sphere
A sphere is round like a ball or marble. It has no flat faces, no vertices, and no edges.

Cylinder
A cylinder has two circular faces. A cylinder can look like a can or pipe.

Cones
A cone has one circular face. Think of an ice cream cone or a party hat.

Can you find something that is a sphere?

Footprints

A footprint is an outline of a foot. Different shaped feet make different kinds of footprints.

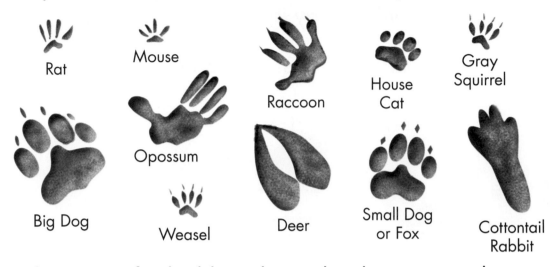

Rat

Mouse

Raccoon

House Cat

Gray Squirrel

Big Dog

Opossum

Weasel

Deer

Small Dog or Fox

Cottontail Rabbit

A footprint of a building shows the shape, or outline, of the bottom floor.

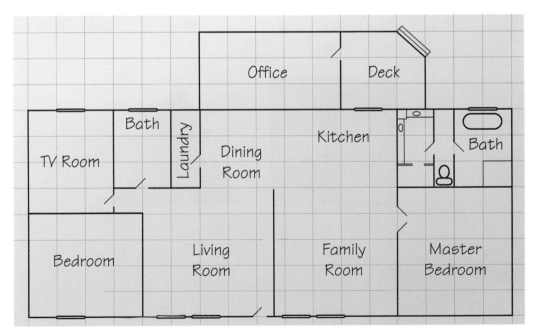

**When do you see your footprints?
What do they look like?**

Geoblock Footprints

A footprint of a Geoblock is an outline of one of its faces. The same block can have several different footprints, depending on which way it is turned.

For example, this triangular prism has 3 footprints.

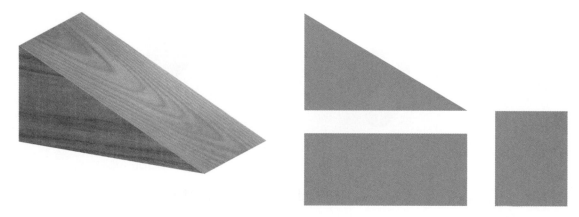

This pyramid has two footprints.

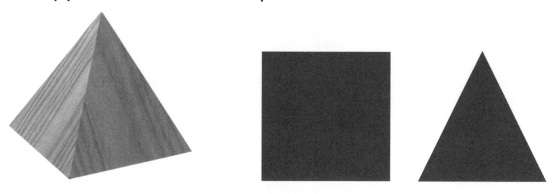

 Can you draw a footprint of this Geoblock?

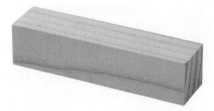

Building with 3-D Shapes

These first graders made a town with 3-D shapes. They also drew 2-D plans of all the buildings in the town. A 2-D plan helps people build the right 3-D building. It can also help them fix the building if it falls down.

Here are some examples of 2-D plans and 3-D buildings:

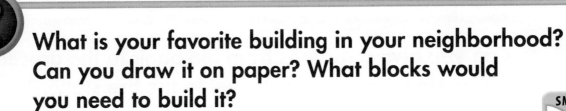

What is your favorite building in your neighborhood? Can you draw it on paper? What blocks would you need to build it?

Giving Directions

Some first graders made a block town in their classroom. Here is a map of their town.

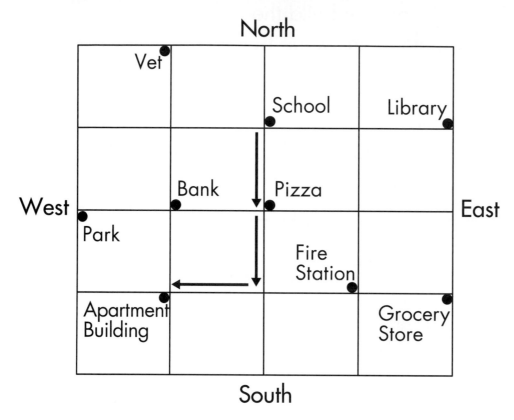

Here are directions from the school to the apartment building.

Start: School
Turn south.
Walk south 2 blocks.
Turn west.
Walk west 1 block.

End: Apartment Building

Can you give directions from the bank to the grocery store? How about from the vet to the fire station?

Measurement

Math Words
• measurement

Measurement can tell you how long, how heavy, or how tall a thing is, or how much space it takes up. You have already taken many measurements. Your height, your weight, and your shoe size are all different kinds of measurement.

We will practice measuring the lengths of objects and the lengths of distances. We will find out how long and how far different things are.

This student is 48 inches tall. This is a measurement of her height.

Measuring Objects

Look around the room. There are many objects and they can all be measured. The measurements can be compared.

What is the longest object you see?
What is the shortest?
Are there any objects that are close in size?
How can you tell whether two objects are exactly the same size?

Measuring objects is important to make sure that things are the right size.

My shoe is longer than my baby brother's shoe.

Length

When you measure length, you measure the long part of an object.

If you are measuring carefully, you should get the same answer each time you measure the same length.

The length of this vase

The length of this book

The length of this desk

Unit

A unit is what you use to measure. When you have finished measuring, count how many units you have used.

Units of paper clips:

This book is 8 paper clips long.

Units of one-inch tiles:

This book is 15 tiles long.

Units of pencils:

This book is 2 pencils long.

If you use different units to measure the same object, the number of units may be different, but the object is still the same length.

Measuring with Units

(page 1 of 2)

If you measure carefully, you will get the same number each time you measure the same object. To measure carefully, make sure that the units line up in a straight line and touch at the edges.

Kira used paper clips to measure her pen. She kept getting different numbers.

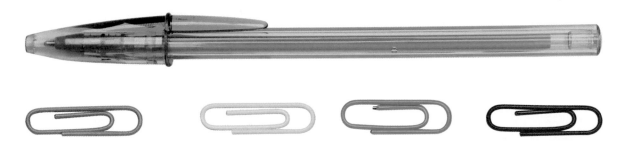

Kira first measured 4 paper clips. Then she noticed that she had left space between the units. She forgot to cover the whole length of the pen.

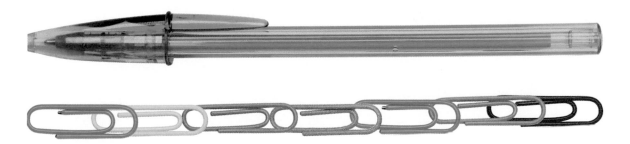

Then Kira counted 7 paper clips but she noticed that the paper clips overlapped.

Measuring with Units

(page 2 of 2)

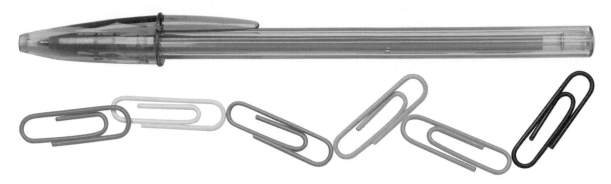

Next, Kira counted 6 paper clips. She noticed that the units were in a zigzag, not a straight line.

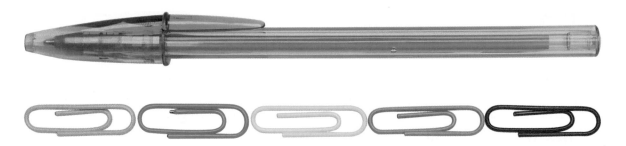

Finally, Kira measured 5 paper clips. She tried again and got the same answer.

 Which measurement do you think is correct? Why?

Inch

An inch is a unit that people can use to measure how long something is.

This line is one inch long. _____

There are many tools we can use to measure in inches.

This tile is 1 inch on each side:

This pencil is 5 inches long:

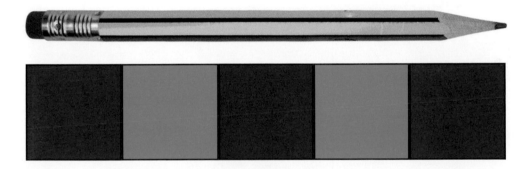

 How many inches long is this pencil?

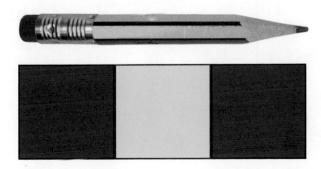

Partial Units (page 1 of 2)

Sometimes when we measure an object, its length falls between two units. There are many ways to talk about this.

Some children measured this pencil with inch tiles.

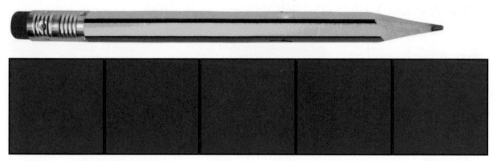

Here is what they said.

The pencil is a little more than 4 tiles long.

It is a little less than 5 inches long.

The pencil is between 4 and 5 inches long.

It is 4 and a half inches long.

Partial Units (page 2 of 2)

All of these ways are right! If you want to talk about something exactly between two whole units you can say it is all of the full units and one half of the last one.

This is how mathematicians write one half: 1/2 $\frac{1}{2}$

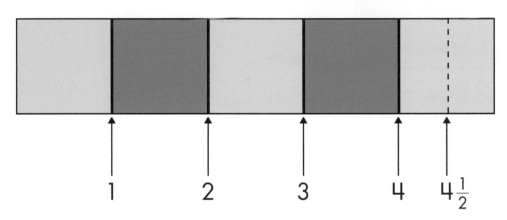

1   2   3   4 $4\frac{1}{2}$

The pencil is $4\frac{1}{2}$ units long.

 How long is the pencil?

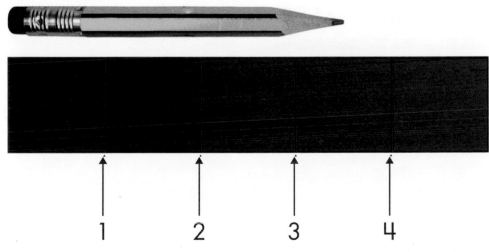

1   2   3   4

At Least

Math Words
• **at least**

At least means "as long as" or "longer than."
For example, if you need a pencil that is at least 4
inches long, it can be 4, 5, 6, or more inches long.

These pencils are at least 4 inches long.

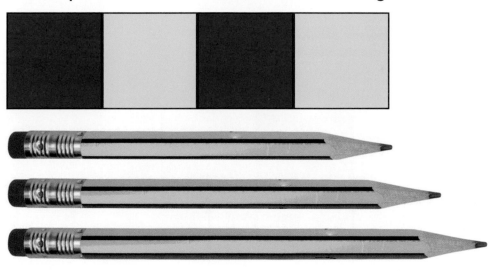

These pencils are not 4 inches long.

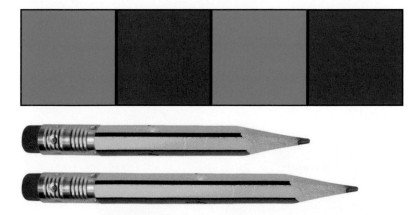

Measuring Distances

Distance is the length between one place and another.

Look at where you are sitting and the nearest door. There is a distance between you and the door. Think about your home and your school. This is a distance you travel every day.

How do you travel a short distance? Did you ever go very far away from home? How did you travel?

Measuring distance is important to find out how far away or close together things are.

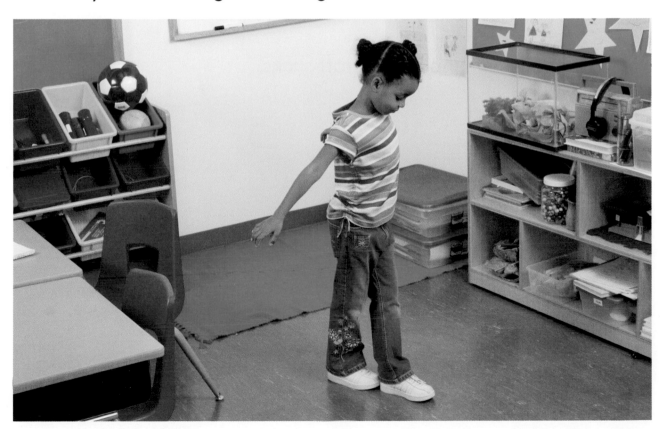

How Far?

Rosa wondered how far her pets could jump.
So she measured the distance that each could jump.
She marked where they started and where they
landed. Then she used craft sticks to measure.

Her frog jumped 10 craft sticks.

Her rabbit jumped 8 craft sticks.

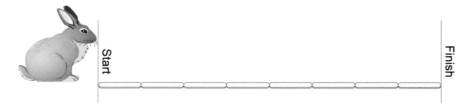

Her grasshopper jumped $6\frac{1}{2}$ craft sticks.

Her mouse jumped 5 craft sticks.

 Did the frog or the rabbit jump farther?

Comparing Measurements: How Much Farther?

Now that Rosa knows how far all of her pets jump, she can compare their jumps.

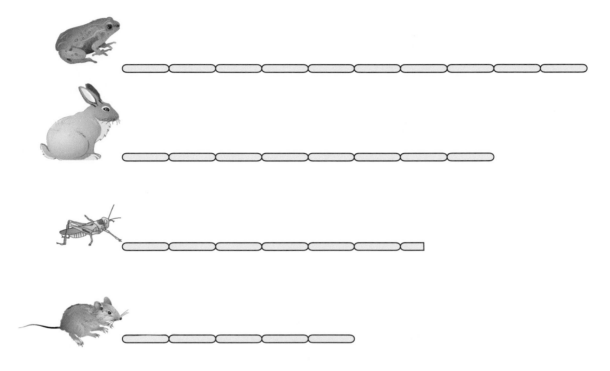

This distance shows how much farther the frog jumped.

The frog jumped 2 craft sticks farther than the rabbit.

How much farther did the frog jump than the mouse? How much farther did the grasshopper jump than the mouse?

Ordered Lists

Rosa organized the jumps in an ordered list from longest to shortest.

The jump on the top of the list is the longest, or farthest, distance.

The jump on the bottom of the list is the shortest distance.

Animal Jumps

Longest	Frog	10 craft sticks
Next Longest	Rabbit	8 craft sticks
Next Longest	Grasshopper	$6\frac{1}{2}$ craft sticks
Shortest	Mouse	5 craft sticks

Comparing Measurements: How Much Longer?

To compare the lengths of these two fish, line up one end and measure how much longer one is than the other.

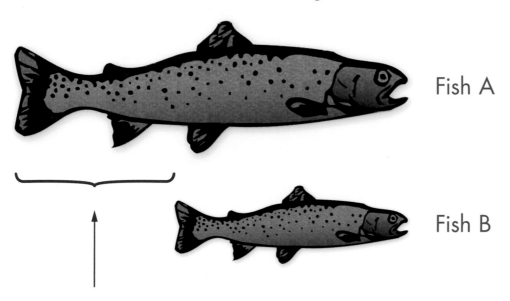

Fish A

Fish B

This distance shows how much longer Fish A is than Fish B.

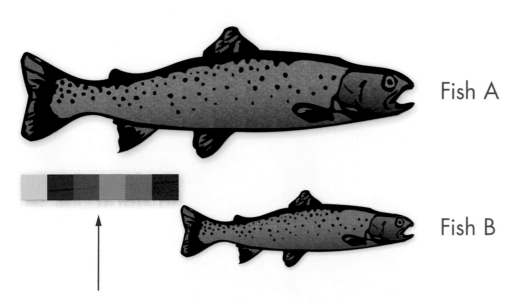

Fish A

Fish B

Fish A is 6 squares longer than Fish B.

Games Chart

	Use in Unit	Page
Collect 20 Together	1	**G1**
Compare	1	**G2**
Compare Dots	1	**G3**
Counters in a Cup	3	**G4**
Dot Addition	3	**G5**
Double Compare	1	**G6**
Double Compare Dots	1	**G7**
Fill the Hexagons	2	**G8**
Five-in-a-Row	1	**G9**
Five-in-a-Row: Subtraction	3	**G10**
Five-in-a-Row with Three Cards	6	**G11**
Guess My Rule	4	**G12**
Heads and Tails	1	**G13**
How Many Am I Hiding?	1	**G14**
Make 10	6	**G15**
Make a Train	7	**G16**
Missing Numbers	3	**G18**
Roll and Record	1	**G19**
Roll and Record: Subtraction	3	**G20**
Roll Tens	8	**G21**
Ten Plus	8	**G22**
Tens Go Fish	6	**G23**
Ten Turns	8	**G24**
Three Towers of 10	6	**G25**

Collect 20 Together

You need

- dot cube

- counters

Play with a partner. Work together.

1 Player 1 rolls the dot cube and takes that many counters.

2 Player 2 rolls the dot cube and takes that many counters.

3 After each turn, count how many counters you have.

4 Keep playing. Players work together to collect 20 counters.

5 The game is over when you have 20 counters together.

More Ways to Play

- Play with 2 dot cubes.

- Play with 1 dot cube and 1 number cube.

- Play *Collect 25 Together* or *Collect 30 Together*.

- Try to collect *exactly* 20 counters.

Compare

You need

- deck of Primary Number Cards (without Wild Cards)

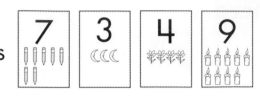

Play with a partner.

1. Deal the cards facedown.

2. Both players turn over the top card.

3. The player with the larger number says "Me!" and takes the cards. If the cards are the same, both players turn over another card.

4. Keep turning over cards. Each time, the player with the larger number says "Me!" and takes the cards.

5. The game is over when there are no more cards to turn over.

More Ways to Play

- The player with the **smaller** number says "Me!"
- Play with 3 players.
- Play with the Wild Cards. A Wild Card can be any number.

Compare Dots

You need

- Dot Cards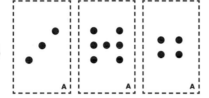

Play with a partner.

1. Deal the cards facedown.

2. Both players turn over the top card.

3. The player with more dots says "Me!" and takes the cards. If the cards are the same, each player turns over another card.

4. Keep turning over cards. Each time, the player with more dots says "Me!" and takes the cards.

5. The game is over when there are no more cards to turn over.

More Ways to Play

- The player with **fewer** dots says "Me!"
- Play with 3 players.

Counters in a Cup

You need

- 8–12 counters

- cup

- recording sheet

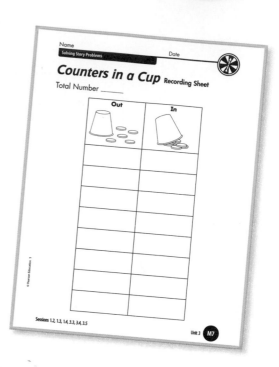

Play with a partner.

1. Decide how many counters to play with. Both players write this number on their recording sheets.

2. Count out that many counters.

3. Player 1 hides some of the counters under a cup.

4. Player 2 tells how many are hidden.

5. Player 1 removes the cup.

6. Both players count the counters that were under the cup and record that number.

7. Keep playing with the same set of counters. Take turns being Player 1 and Player 2.

8. The game is over when the grid is full.

Dot Addition

You need

- deck of Dot Addition Cards

- 3 gameboards (one per player and one to play on)

Play with a partner.

1 Deal 4 rows of 5 cards, with the dots facing up.

2 Player 1 finds cards that combine to make one of the numbers on the gameboard.

3 Both players record the combination.

4 Player 2 finds cards that combine to make another number on the gameboard.

5 Both players record the combination.

6 The game is over when the gameboard is full.

More Ways to Play

- Play with different gameboards.
- Use each card only once.
- Play again, with the same gameboard. Try to find a different way to make each number.

Double Compare

You need

- deck of Primary Number Cards (without Wild Cards)

Play with a partner.

1. Deal the cards facedown.

2. Both players turn over their top two cards.

3. The player with the larger total says "Me!" and takes the cards. If the totals are the same, both players turn over two more cards.

4. Keep turning over two cards. Each time, the player with the larger total says "Me!" and takes the cards.

5. The game is over when there are no more cards to turn over.

More Ways to Play

- The player with the **smaller** total says "Me!"
- Play with 3 players.
- Play with the Wild Cards. A Wild Card can be any number.

Double Compare Dots

You need

- Dot Cards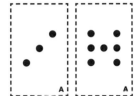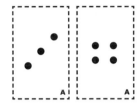

Play with a partner.

1 Deal the cards facedown.

2 Both players turn over their top two cards.

3 The player with cards having more dots says "Me!" and takes the cards. If both pairs of cards have the same number of dots, both players turn over two more cards.

4 Keep turning over two cards. Each time, the player with more dots says "Me!" and takes the cards.

5 The game is over when there are no more cards in the deck.

More Ways to Play

- The player whose cards have **fewer** dots says "Me!"

- Play with 3 players.

Fill the Hexagons

You need

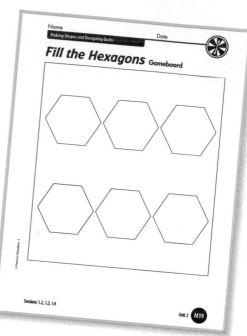

- pattern blocks
- 2 pattern block cubes
- gameboard (1 per player)

Play with a partner. Work together.

1 Player 1 rolls the pattern block cubes.

2 Player 1 places those pattern blocks anywhere on the gameboard. Once a block is placed, it cannot be moved.

3 Player 2 rolls the pattern block cubes.

4 Player 2 places those pattern blocks anywhere on the gameboard.

5 Players 1 and 2 continue playing, repeating steps 1–4.

6 The game is over when one player has covered all of the hexagons on the gameboard with blocks.

Five-in-a-Row

You need

- 2 dot cubes
- 20 counters
- gameboard

Name _____ Date _____
How Many of Each?

Five-in-a-Row Gameboard A

2	3	4	5	6
6	7	7	8	9
10	11	12	11	10
9	8	7	7	6
6	5	4	3	2

M26   Unit 1
Sessions 3.2, 3.4, 3.5, 3.6

Play with a partner. Work together.

1. Player 1 rolls two cubes.

2. Player 1 adds ⬛ + ⬛.

3. Player 1 covers that sum on the gameboard.

4. Player 2 takes a turn, following steps 1–3.

5. If the sum is already covered, roll again.

6. The game is over when all of the numbers in one row are covered. The numbers can go across ▭▭▭▭▭, down ▯, or corner to corner.

More Ways to Play

- Play with different gameboards.
- Play with 1 dot cube and 1 number cube. ⬛ 2
- Play with 2 number cubes. 3 5

Five-in-a-Row: Subtraction

You need

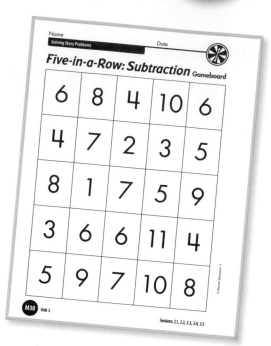

- 7–12 number cube

- dot cube

- 20 counters

- gameboard

Play with a partner. Work together.

1. Player 1 rolls two cubes.

2. Player 1 subtracts the smaller number from the larger number.

3. Player 1 covers that number on the gameboard.

4. Player 2 takes a turn, following steps 1–3.

5. If the number is already covered, roll again.

6. The game is over when all of the numbers in one row are covered. The numbers can go across ⬜⬜⬜⬜⬜, down ⬜, or corner to corner.

Five-in-a-Row with Three Cards

You need

- deck of Primary Number Cards (without Wild Cards)

- 20 counters
- gameboard

Name
Number Games and Crayon Puzzles   **Date**

Five-in-a-Row with Three Cards
Gameboard A

2	4	6	8	10
10	10	12	12	14
16	18	20	19	17
15	13	11	11	11
9	9	7	5	3

M42 Unit 6   Sessions 3.1, 3.3, 3.6, 3.7

Play with a partner. Work together.

1. Turn over the top 3 cards.

2. Player 1 chooses a sum to cover on the gameboard. Choose any sum you can make with 2 of the numbers.

   $3 + 7 = ⑩$ $7 + 1 = ⑧$ $3 + 1 = ④$

3. Turn over three more cards.

4. Player 2 chooses a sum to cover on the gameboard.

5. Keep playing. If all of the sums are covered, pick 3 new cards.

6. The game is over when all of the numbers in one row are covered. The numbers can go across ⬚⬚⬚⬚⬚, down ▯, or corner to corner.

More Ways to Play

- Play with different gameboards.
- Play with the Wild Cards. A Wild Card can be any number.
- Turn over 5 cards on each turn. Choose any sum you can make with 2 of the numbers.

Guess My Rule

You need

- 20–25 buttons

- sorting mats

Play with a group of 2–4 players.

1. Player 1 chooses a rule that fits some of the buttons and writes it on a piece of paper.

2. Player 1 puts two buttons that fit the rule on the "These Fit My Rule" paper and two buttons that don't fit the rule on the "These Don't Fit My Rule" paper.

3. Player 2 puts a button where he or she thinks it belongs.

4. Players take turns placing buttons.

5. After each player has placed 3 buttons, players may try to guess the rule on their next turn.

6. The game is over once the rule has been guessed correctly.

7. Play again. Another player chooses the rule.

Heads and Tails

You need

- 8–12 pennies

- recording sheet

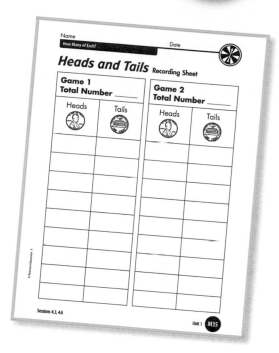

Play alone.

1 Decide how many pennies to play with. Record this number on the recording sheet.

2 Drop the pennies.

3 Count how many pennies are heads  and how many pennies are tails .

4 Record the two numbers on the recording sheet.

5 Keep dropping the pennies and recording how they land.

6 The game is over when the grid is full.

How Many Am I Hiding?

You need

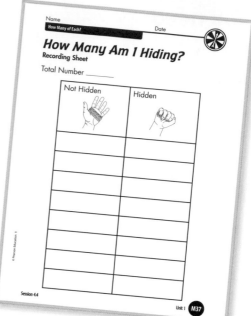

- 8–12 connecting cubes
- recording sheet

Name _____ Date _____

How Many of Each?

How Many Am I Hiding?
Recording Sheet

Total Number _____

Not Hidden	Hidden

© Pearson Education 1

Session 4.4   Unit 1 M37

Play with a partner.

1 Decide how many cubes to play with. Both players write this number on their recording sheets.

2 Make a tower with that many cubes.

3 Player 1 hides some of the cubes.

4 Player 2 tells how many cubes are hidden.

5 Player 1 shows the hidden cubes.

6 Both players count how many were hidden and then record that number on their recording sheets.

7 Keep playing with the same tower. Take turns being Player 1 and Player 2.

8 The game is over when the grid is full.

More Ways to Play

- Play with 5 cubes of one color and 5 cubes of another color.

Make 10

You need

- deck of Primary Number Cards (without Wild Cards)
- blank sheet of paper

Play with a partner.

1 Deal 4 rows of 5 cards, with the numbers showing.

2 Player 1 finds two cards that make 10. Player 1 takes the cards and records the combination of 10.

3 Replace the missing cards with 2 cards from the deck.

4 Player 2 finds two cards that make 10. Player 2 takes the cards and records the combination of 10.

5 Replace the missing cards.

6 Keep taking turns finding two cards that make 10 and recording.

7 The game is over when there are no more cards or there are no more cards that make 10.

More Ways to Play

- Play with the Wild Cards. A Wild Card can be any number.
- Replace the cards *only* when there are no more pairs that make 10.
- Find more than 2 cards that make 10.

Make a Train (page 1 of 2)

You need

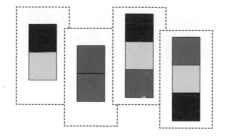

- *Make a Train* cards

- Color Cube

- connecting cubes

- a bag

- sheet of paper (or paper plate or a box) to be the "depot"

Play with a partner.

1 Each player draws a *Make a Train* card from the bag. Players use connecting cubes to make what is on the card.

If Player 1 draws a red-yellow *Make a Train* card, he or she makes a car with a red cube and a yellow cube.

If Player 2 draws a red-green-yellow *Make a Train* card, he or she makes a red-green-yellow car with those colored cubes.

Make a Train (page 2 of 2)

2 Player 1 rolls the Color Cube.

If the color rolled matches a color on either of the two trains, Player 1 takes a cube of that color and puts it in the "depot" (piece of paper, paper plate, or box). The depot is where the cubes are held until they can be made into cars.

If a star is rolled, the player can take any color.

If the color rolled is not in either of the two trains, the same player rolls again.

3 Player 2 rolls the Color Cube, and places a cube of that color in the depot if either train has that color. The players check to see whether a complete car can be made for either train from the cubes in the depot.

4 Players continue to take turns and work together to make both trains 12 cubes long.

5 The game is over when there are two trains that are 12 cubes long.

Missing Numbers

You need

1	2	3	4	5	6	7	8	9	10
11	12	13	14	15	16	17	18	19	20
21	22	23	24	25	26	27	28	29	30
31	32	33	34	35	36	37	38	39	40
41	42	43	44	45	46	47	48	49	50
51	52	53	54	55	56	57	58	59	60
61	62	63	64	65	66	67	68	69	70
71	72	73	74	75	76	77	78	79	80
81	82	83	84	85	86	87	88	89	90
91	92	93	94	95	96	97	98	99	100

- 100 chart

- 10 pennies

- recording sheet

Play with a partner.

1. Player 1 covers five numbers on the 100 chart with pennies.

2. Player 2 figures out which numbers are missing.

3. Both players record the missing numbers on their recording sheets.

4. Remove the pennies. Check your work.

5. Take turns hiding the numbers.

6. The game is over when the recording sheet is full.

More Ways to Play

- Cover 10 more numbers.
- Play with a small group.

Roll and Record

You need

- 2 dot cubes
- recording sheet

Play alone.

1 Roll 2 cubes.

2 Add the numbers. ▢ + ▢

3 Write the sum on the recording sheet.

4 The game is over when one column is full.

More Ways to Play

- Play with 1 dot cube and 1 number cube. ▢ **6**
- Play with 2 number cubes. **5** **4**

Roll and Record: Subtraction

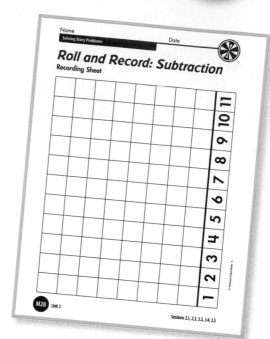

You need

- 7–12 number cube

- dot cube

- recording sheet

Play alone.

1 Roll the 2 cubes.

2 Subtract the smaller number from the larger number.

3 Record the answer on the recording sheet.

4 The game is over when one column is full.

Roll Tens

You need

- number cube
- dot cube
- 30 connecting cubes
- 30 mat

Play with a partner. Work together.

1 Player 1 rolls the dot cube and the number cube.

2 Player 1 adds **3** and ⚃, and puts that many connecting cubes in a row on the mat. A row can only have 10 cubes. If cubes are left over, start a new row.

3 Player 2 rolls the dot cube and the number cube.

4 Player 2 adds **1** and ⚄, and puts that many connecting cubes in a row on the mat.

5 The game is over when the mat is full.

More Ways to Play

- Play on the 50 Mat.
  Use 50 connecting cubes.

- Play on the 100 Mat.
  Use 100 connecting cubes.

50 MAT   **100 MAT**

Ten Plus

You need

- deck of Primary Number Cards (without Wild Cards)

- 20 cubes

- recording sheet

Play with a partner.

1. Turn over the top two cards.

2. Make an equivalent expression, using the two numbers from the cards and 10.

   $5 + 8 = 10 + \boxed{}$

3. Both players record $5 + 8$ in the correct column on the recording sheet.

4. Turn over the next 2 cards and repeat steps 2–3.

5. The game is over when one column of the recording sheet is filled.

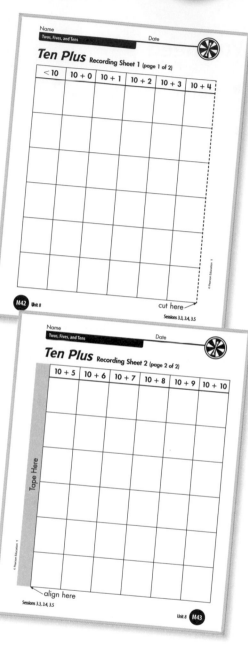

Tens Go Fish

You need

- deck of Primary Number Cards (without Wild Cards)
- sheet of paper

Play with a partner.

1. Each player is dealt 5 cards from the Primary Number Card deck.

2. Each player looks for pairs from his or her cards that make 10. Players put down the pairs of cards that make 10, and they draw new cards to replace them from the Primary Number Card deck.

3. Players take turns asking each other for a card that will make 10 with a card in their own hands.

   If a player gets the card, he or she puts the pair down and picks a new card from the deck.

   If a player does not get the card, the player must "Go fish" and pick a new card from the deck.

   If the new card from the deck makes 10 with a card in the player's hand, he or she puts the pair of cards down and takes another card.

   If a player runs out of cards, the player picks two new cards. A player's turn is over when no more pairs can be made that make 10.

4. The game is over when there are no more cards.

5. At the end of the game, players record their combinations of 10.

Ten Turns

You need

- number cube

- 60 counters

- *Ten Turns* Recording Sheet
  (1 per player)

Play with a partner. Work together.

1 Player 1 rolls the number cube.

2 Player 1 makes a group of
counters the same number
as the one that was rolled.

3 Both players record the number of counters
in the group.

4 Player 2 rolls the number cube.

5 Player 2 adds that number of counters to
the group.

6 Both players record the new number of
counters in the group.

7 Players repeat steps 1–6.

8 The game is over after 10 turns.

Three Towers of 10

You need

- dot cube

- 30 connecting cubes per player, in 2 colors

- crayons in 2 colors

- recording sheet

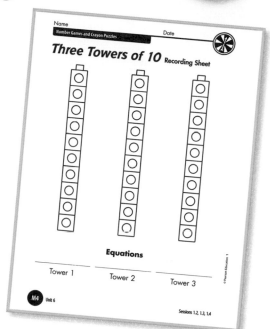

Play with a partner. Work together.

1. Each player picks a color of cubes.

2. Player 1 rolls and makes a tower with that many cubes.

3. Player 2 rolls and takes that many cubes.

4. Player 2 adds the cubes to the tower. A tower can have only 10 cubes. Start a new tower with any extra cubes.

5. The game is over when there are 3 towers of 10 cubes.

6. Both players record. Show how many cubes of each color there are in each tower. Write an equation for each tower.

More Ways to Play

- Make 5 towers of 10.
- Make 3 towers of 15.
- Play with 2 dot cubes.
- Play with 1 dot cube and 1 number cube.
- Play with 2 number cubes.

Illustrations

12, 17, 24, 62, 89, 107   Jeff Grunewald
39, 53–57, 104   Thomas Gagliano

Photographs

Every effort has been made to secure permission and provide appropriate credit for photographic material. The publisher deeply regrets any omission and pledges to correct errors called to its attention in subsequent editions.

Unless otherwise acknowledged, all photographs are the property of Scott Foresman, a division of Pearson Education.

Photo locators denoted as follows: Top (T), Center (C), Bottom (B), Left (L), Right (R), Background (Bkgd)

Cover ©Steve Allen/Alamy Images; **21** Getty Images; **34** Getty Images; **56** Getty Images; **57** Stockdisc; **59** (BR) Jupiter Images, (BL) ©Stockbyte; **70** Roy Ooms/Masterfile Corporation; **83** (BR) Getty Images, (CL,C) ©AbleStock/Index Open, (BC) NASA, (TC) Goodshoot/Jupiter Images; **95** © Stockbyte; **99** Stockdisc